All the tracks from the album arranged for voice, piano & guitar

DINA CARROLL

SO CLOSE

GW00722714

Wise Publications

London / New York / Paris / Sydney / Copenhagen / Madrid

Exclusive Distributors:

Music Sales Limited
8/9 Frith Street, London W1V 5TZ, England.

Music Sales Pty Limited
120 Rothschild Avenue, Rosebery, NSW 2018, Australia.

Order No. AM91985
ISBN 0-7119-4101-7
This book © Copyright 1994 by Wise Publications.

Music arranged by Roger Day.
Music processed by MSS Studios.

Your Guarantee of Quality:
As publishers, we strive to produce every book to the highest commercial standards.

The music has been freshly engraved and, whilst endeavouring to retain the
original running order of the album, the book has been carefully designed to
minimise awkward page turns and to make playing from it a real pleasure.

Particular care has been given to specifying acid-free, neutral-sized paper made from
pulps which have not been elemental chlorine bleached. This pulp is from farmed sustainable
forests and was produced with special regard for the environment.

Throughout, the printing and binding have been planned to ensure a sturdy,
attractive publication which should give years of enjoyment.

If your copy fails to meet our high standards, please inform us and we will gladly replace it.

Music Sales' complete catalogue describes thousands of titles and
is available in full colour sections by subject, direct from Music Sales Limited.
Please state your areas of interest and send a cheque/postal order for £1.50 for postage to:
Music Sales Limited, Newmarket Road, Bury St. Edmunds, Suffolk IP33 3YB.

Printed in the United Kingdom by
J.B. Offset Printers (Marks Tey) Limited, Marks Tey, Essex.

Special Kind Of Love

Words & Music by David Cole & Robert Clivilles

1. Re-mem-ber the day
2. *(see block lyric)*

that we first met, how you drove me craz - y.

we ___ got a spec - ial kind ___ of love. ___

You know, you know, you know that

Verse 2:
You make me happy whenever I'm blue,
I can count on you
To groove me and release my frustration
And turn my bad into something good.
You give me love incredible,
So special is the love we share and we,
We belong together,
All the possibilities.

They say that nothing lasts forever,
But we got it going on.
We'll hold on through stormy weather
With a love so strong.
(To Chorus)

Hold On

Words & Music by Dina Carroll & Nigel Lowis

1. See that bro-ther on the street, he's do-in'

2. *(see block lyric)*

fine, Yet all the peo-ple that he sees,

They're all so blind. _____ 'Cause

he's got _ his prob - lems, yes he's got _ his cross _ to bear

like so man - y oth - ers _ in life, do they real - ly

care? _____ Got - ta live your life the way _ you choose,

learn from the chang - es you __ go through and hold __ on. __

(You've got to) deal with the prob - lems that __ you find, __

it - 'll get bet - ter the more __ you try __ to hold __ on, __ hold

on. __

Coda

D.%.al Coda

We've

Got-ta live your life the way — you choose,

Repeat ad lib. to fade

on.

Verse 2:
See me walking down the street,
I'm doing fine.
Yet all the people that I meet,
They think they know my mind.

But I've got my problems,
Yes I've got my own price to pay.
Like so many others,
I'm still trying to find my own way. *(To chorus)*

Verse 3: (D.S.)
We've all got our problems,
We've all got our own price to pay.
Like so many others,
We're still trying to find our own way. *(To chorus)*

This Time

Words & Music by Dina Carroll & Nigel Lowis

1. Lone - ly, _____ you on my mind, _____ how could I let you go, _
2. (see block lyric)

all that we've been _ through. I still _____ need you

next to me. _____

I said so ma - ny things _

This time ___ it could be ___ so com - plete. ___ It's time ___ for us to be to - geth - er, now I know what you mean ___ to ___ me.

No - one could hold ___ me, ___ no - one could have told ___ me ___ that I would be feel - ing ___ this way.

The day's get-ting long - er, ____ the feel-ing is strong - er, ____ put an

end to ____ this pain right ____ a - way. ____

D.%.al Coda

Coda

me.   I'm still   want-ing you, need-ing you, miss-ing you, feel-ing you

Verse 2:
Now that I understand
Through all this loneliness, I need no other man,
So here I am,
I'm still needing you.
As you were leaving I knew I was to blame,
But I'm not gonna beg you to come back and stay.

So make up your mind now 'cause it's all up to you,
'Cause we owe it to ourselves to see this through.

Verse 3 (D.S.)
Oh what a fool I must have been
To lose the love that you were giving me.

Falling

Words & Music by Dina Carroll & Nigel Lowis

23

heart, tell me that you're for real.

Fall-ing and there's

Verse 2:
It's not that I was looking for someone
To share my life.
I thought it would be such a waste of time
Until I found you.

Well I've realised
That I just can't disguise how I feel.
So don't be surprised
When I look in your eyes and reveal.

So Close

Words & Music by Dina Carroll & Nigel Lowis

1. I've known a - bout all your faults, — some - how they nev - er de - ter _____ me, _____
2. *(see block lyric)*

and there are times when we talk, _____ you real - ly know how to soothe

close ___ to you, ___ (where I wan-na be, you and me) and it

feels so ___ good ___ so ___ close ___ to you, ___ feels so ___ good.

So good to me, ___ so good to me, ___

28

Verse 2:
Sometimes you say that I'm cold,
Don't ever think that you'll lose me.
I'll never tire of your hold,
'Cause you know just how to move me.
Well you're aware as I am too,
That there's good and bad in the things we do.
But after all is said and done,
There's nothing sweeter.

Ain't No Man

Words & Music by Dina Carroll & Nigel Lowis

1. I just can't con-trol how I feel a - bout
2. *(see block lyric)*

_ you, _ and I'm so sur - prised with the way I act, _ when you're _ a - round.

I know they nev-er see all the things that I ___ see, ___ they don't un-der-

stand just what it is ___ that we ___ have found. ___

Well I don't ___ care ___

man _ makes me feel like you _ do, there ain't no man _ that I've ev - er found.

2. I sim - ply love the

Verse 2:
I simply love the times that we spend together
And I love the things that you say to me when we're alone.
There isn't any doubt in the way I'm feeling
And I hope the way that I'm feeling now will never go.

Well I don't care...(etc. as verse 1)

Express

Words & Music by Dina Carroll & Nigel Lowis

never tell my momma just what I felt. So ease your mind and just

let your inner feelings show. Let's make the

time and just let your inhibitions flow. You've gotta

A7

do what you wanna, see who you wanna,

37

2. Watch- ing you

N.C.

D.%.al Coda

3. There may be

⊕ Coda

A7

G#7 4 fr.   A7

G#7 4 fr.

Vocals ad lib. to fade

Verse 2:
Watching you stare gets me thinking
That if I don't make a move sometime this evening,
I'm gonna lose
All the things that momma told me I should never do.

Verse 3:
There may be times when you're drinking
When your mouth doesn't always say what your body's thinking.
But it feels oh so good,
Oh like you know it should.

Heaven Sent

Words & Music by Dina Carroll & Nigel Lowis

1. There are days I get so tired of be-ing me, ___
2. (see block lyric)

there are days I just can't face re-a-li-ty. ___

And deal-ing with peo - ple — that I just don't — wan - na see, ——— gets me

think-ing 'bout — you and me. — In my mind I dream of

how I wan-na be, — that's not the on - ly way I keep my san - i - ty. —

'Cause giv - en time — I know ev - en - tu - al - ly, ——— I will

42

sa- tis- fied. ___ I

know I've ___ got you and ___ that you'll see ___ me through ___ (love), it's all I

need from ___ you, ____ (Your love) it's what takes _____ me ___ through, ___

(Mine) ___ yes you're mine, ____ (Mine) well yes you're mine. _____

Heav - en must have sent you to me. ____

Don't think I ____

____ don't ___ know _____ 'cause

you came __ a - long, you made me __ so strong, ____ showed me __ how sweet life can

be.

(Your

love), it's all I need from — you, ——— (Your

Verse 2:
There are days I just can't find the energy,
It seems so hard to find a little harmony.
You give the strength, you give it right back to me
When I need to get by.

I don't have to question the things that you do,
There's never a doubt in my mind about you.
You're the one choice I've made in my life,
I'm so satisfied, I'm so satisfied.

You'll Never Know

Words & Music by Dina Carroll & Nigel Lowis

1. You'll _____ nev - er know _____ all _ the pain that I was feel-
2.3. *(see block lyric)*

- ing. _ You'll nev - er see _____ all the tears _ that I've cried.

Verse 2:
You never told me
That you would be leaving.
I realised half the time
It was me you were deceiving

(What were the reasons)
Why you never said goodbye
(Just implications)
As to why you never never never...

Verse 3:
8 bars instrumental
(What were the reasons)
Why you never said goodbye
(Just implications)
As to why you never never never...

Don't Be A Stranger

Words & Music by Coral Gordon & Geoff Gurd

1.I should-n't be a-lone with you— to-night,— de-si-re was too strong to put— up a fight.——— I don't un-der-stand— the way— I feel,— al-though it feels— so right,— I real-ly shouldn't

what I'm gon - na do.___ If on-ly for to - night___ Don't be a stran - ger. I want it

1. all from___ you___ to - night.___

2. all from___ you___ to - night.

Why? I don't know,___ I'm in too

Verse 2:
You're on my mind all of the time,
I really shouldn't stay with you tonight,
But the more and more I think of it, the more it just seems right,
That's why I shouldn't be here tonight.
Now I find I don't know who I really am, I'm lost without a trace,
So take me high, take me low, any how you know, and help me if you can.

Why Did I Let You Go?

Words & Music by Dina Carroll & Nigel Lowis

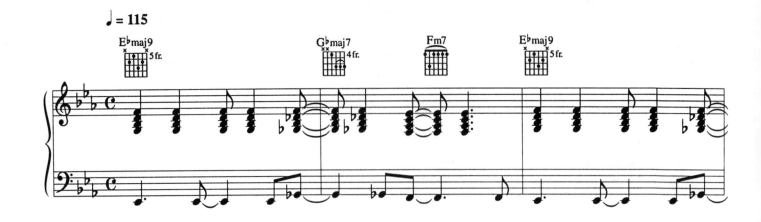

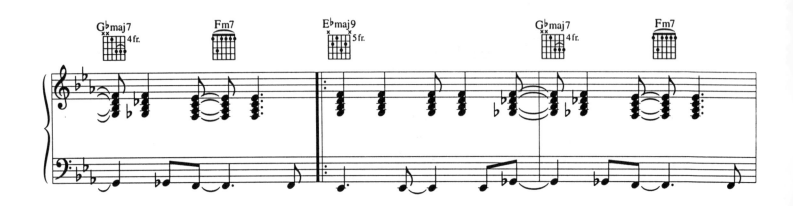

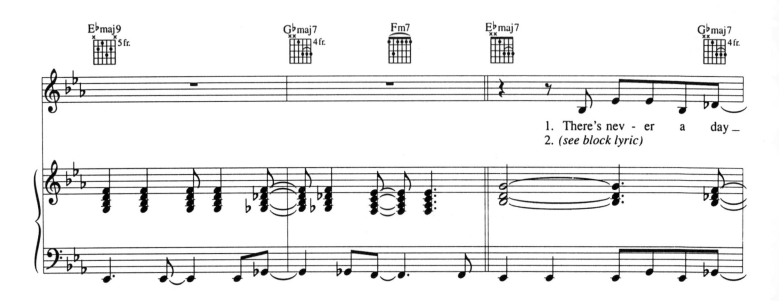

1. There's nev - er a day _
2. *(see block lyric)*

58

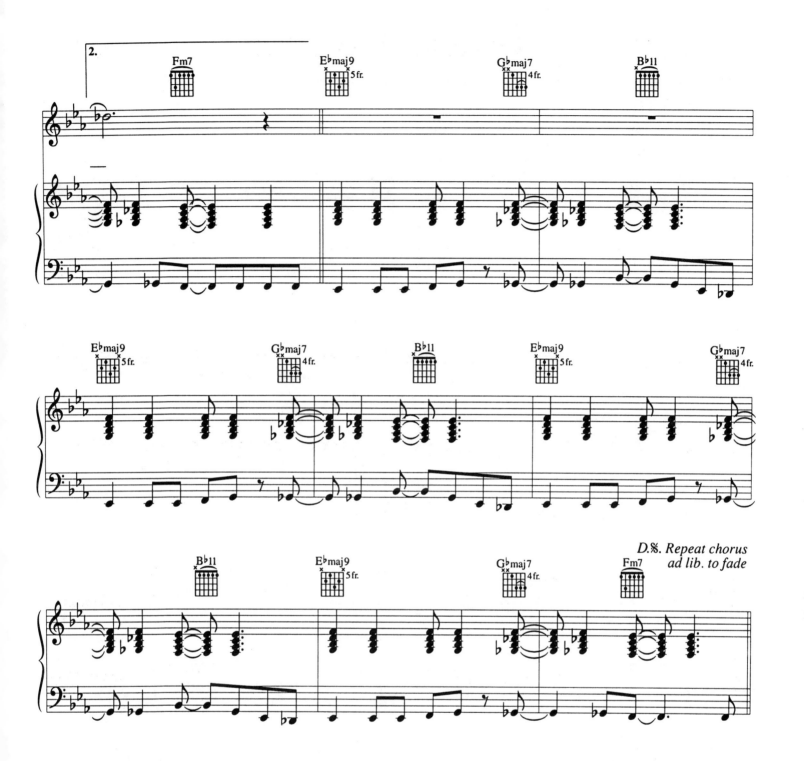

Verse 2:
I may have mistreated you sometime,
But you can't tell me the fault's all mine, all mine.
The empty words that you heard me with
Still run through my mind.
But that won't change the way that I,
That I feel inside.

on D.S.
You told me that you would be leaving me,
You said you'd be gone this time,
The thought of you gone forever
It never, never crossed my mind.

If I Knew You Then

Words & Music by Dina Carroll & Nigel Lowis

Verse 2:
Oh I just can't believe that it took so long for me to see
It's you that makes me so complete.
When we're lying here and I feel that you are so close to me
I know that you are all I need.
Now I know that there ain't nobody who loves me like you do
Now I know I'll never love somebody the way that I love you.

D.S.
Didn't think that I'd meet somebody who loves me like you do,
Didn't think I'd ever love somebody the way that I love you.